Writing Between the Lines

Nolcha Fox

Table of Contents

Acknowledgments

The poems in this book came out of a 30-poems-in-30-days challenge to use two lines/phrases/sentences from published poems as the first and last lines of new poems.

Thanks to:
- *Contemplate* for publishing "Pray and Measure," and "Flight"
- *Doctor Funny* for publishing "Sport"
- *Garden of Neuro* for publishing "Jarred"
- *Fevers of the Mind* for publishing "Postures," Dinner," "Choosing a Direction," "Platform," and "Need All"

Sport

I am a spectator at my own sport.
My sport is evading morphing decay.
I assume the pretzel posture in yoga.
In my mind, I am the instructor,
unjointed and surgically enhanced.
My underwear protests.

*First and last lines from Sandra Cisneros' poem, "At
Fifty I Am Startled to Find I Am in My Splendor"*

Drunk

When the night climbs into my bed,
we drink a glass of brandy.
Sleep goes out for a
good time with the girls.
Sleep is sloshed when she comes back
and I'm not far behind her.
Night calls Dawn for room service
and curls up on the couch.
Sleep and Dawn and I link arms,
our little drunken army
marching out of the night.

First and last lines from Jackson Holbert's poem, "Poem with a Smoke Cloud Hanging in It"

Braided

Peel back the greening leaf
of spring, of childhood.
Reveal the virgin seeds.
Weave rivulets through fresh-turned soil.
Tell me where the flowers lay braided.

First and last lines from Erica Vital-Lazare's poem,
Aguadilla

Dog Days

It floods the forest with loud barks of light,
chases rabbits into shadow burrows,
laps coffee from my cup,
demands I change from robe to jeans
for walk through flowering fields.
It jumps into the muddy creek
and showers me with drops of sun,
the noon, a mystic dog with paws of fire.

*First and last lines from Harindranath Chattopadhyaya's
poem, "Noon"*

Bait

Each of my father's eyes is a globe of brown worms.
Worms are good for bait. But not tonight. The fish don't
bite.
My father's eyes are mirrors reflecting the moon.
My father's eyes are lights on the water.
Fish jump into our laps, jump for his eyes.
That's how I know that fish love to swallow whatever
resembles a lamp.

First and last lines from Hussain Ahmed's poem,
"Cosmology of the Cloud with Baba as the Rain Maker"

Not No

The not-yet of a white realm of nothing left,
a Swiss cheese hole filled with probabilities and mold,
molding time into space into void,
voiding a ticket for a trip not taken,
a no-longer already there, along with the arrival of what
has been.

*First and last lines from Carolyn Forchés poem, "What
Comes"*

Lightning

Blackbird heart with lightning bolts
jolts wings across the darkening sky.
She warbles thunder song to distant mate,
makes nest of broken steel shards
where the flash that shatters night comes to roost.

First and last lines from Amanda Berenguer's poem,
"Avec les gémissements graves du Montévidéen"

City, City

I was like you once, he added, in love with turbulence.
I was a red ball bounced against billboards by
circumstance.
I was a freeway under orange-barrel construction.
My angry commute was eaten by streetlights.
The city is a myth of silence.
The city — the city is where I disappear.

First and last lines from Louise Gluck's poem,
"Aboriginal Landscape"

Lost Ugly

I lost my slippers and face
in the room with cracked walls
that let secrets seep through
into airwaves unheard.
My mistakes, faded and frayed,
hung on wires strung
between drifting clouds.
I thought thoughts ugly as clothespins.

First and last lines from Leslie Sainz' poem, "Sonnet for Ochún"

Platform

His portrait on the frontispiece looks mournfully at
my wandering attention. It sighs each time I lose myself
in vanishing distractions. I promise to remember,
I press flowers in the pages that will crumble into dust.
Books pile higher, they're a tower, they're a city,
they're lost hours, they're a platform constructed
from prayers that didn't require an answer.

First and last lines from George Franklin's poems,
"Rabelais" and "Adam Zagajewski Enters Into Heaven"

Missing Parts

We're all missing parts.
We're all parts missing from somewhere.
We're babies missing the womb,
missing from the womb.
The womb remembers, misses the fullness,
the wholeness she holds in the hollow.

First and last lines from Lisa Allen Ortiz' poem,
"Sternocleidomastoid"

Place

My mother was a place
to base my house of cards,
a road falling off the map,
footsteps to the edge
of a bottomless gorge,
the hand that pushed me
into what could be
as I grew into my own wild country.

*First and last lines from Hayden Saunier's poem, "A
Cartography of Home"*

Hiding

I spent summer afternoons
nowhere to be found.
I was the shadow of trees,
the ripples in the pool,
the cool of the theater.
My only purpose
to move through life unnoticed.

*First and last lines from Elizabeth Onusko's poem,
"Named Storm"*

Need All

In the need-all of snow,
a frozen key to solve the puzzle
of scrambled words with eggs
and bewildered burnt bacon.
Confusion left to simmer,
we dive into our meal,
listening in silence to
the biscuit-breaking sounds.

First and last lines from Tony Ashenden's poem, "The Need-all of Snow"

Dinner

I could rest a dinner set on
the stare you gave me on the bus,
a look to shred cabbage.
My stare back was Jell-O
all a-jitter, we would prick our
fingers trying to pick up the broken
china off the floor.

*First and last lines from Alex Carrigan's poem, "Glass
Earrings"*

Postures

Love's old postures appear
in an old black-and-white movie,
Cigarettes poised to kiss pouting lips.
The close-ups, the longing
of two lovers parting,
The credits roll by
with the spring lethargy of a lover.

First and last lines from Jules Gibbs' poem, "X"

Closed for Business

We allow our lips to remain closed,
two ununited nations
allowing no trade.
We sit in silence
an ice pick couldn't shatter,
to give us a reason to break ourselves.

First and last lines from Alex Carrigan's poem, "After the Ambulance"

Ruins

You will always end up in Roma: I will always remain in you.
I am the rum that wrecks and ruins what you touch.
I am a sandcastle ruined by the waves of your hair.
I will leave Roma without you.
I will find my way alone without you,
even if on every street, I find the ruins of our bodies.

First and last lines from Nathalie Handal's poem, "The City"

Hard Road

What hardens in you keeps you hungry
for steel to sharpen your teeth.
You are the gravel crushed
under the collisions
of metal and lightning,
You are the horizon
the asphalt never meets.
You are lost on a highway
that goes nowhere.
The road ahead turns as dark as your days.

*First and last lines from Virgil Suarez' poem, "Axiom of
the Outsider"*

Jarred

As if the honey could replenish
all that had been plundered.
As if my soul, sold for money,
could find redemption in a jar.
As if my promises were golden
globs of sweetness I could feed
you with a spoon.
As if a jar of honey was an orange
slice of sky.
As if my hands, holding the virgin jar,
could serve as makeshift womb.

*First and last lines from Francesca Moroney's poem, "I
Kept Buying Bottles of Honey"*

Sorrow

Sorrow reeking of poppies & garlic,
he was an overdone serenade
you drowned in wine and rosewater.
He was the caterwaul caught
in a violin string,
dragging his solo behind him.

First and last lines from John Amen's poem, "Conjugal"

Choosing a Direction

She's often found it hard to pick a direction,
to follow a direction after turning left, then right.
She crawls through life, uncertain snail,
no decision is too small to fret about for hours.
Whether to wear purple is a gamble
with the last hours of her life.
Will she choose the gangplank
instead of the roller coaster?

First and last lines from Alex Carrigan's poem, "Four Women Laying Domino Trains"

Stitched

Who am I but the scent of blood
passed down in handmade gown,
fingers pricked to mark the needle
sewing rips together.
Lace and satin frail from lies
that love would last forever,
truth is scissors, brandished, broken,
set aside for mending kit,
stitch-marks where a war once raged.

*First and last lines from Sheree La Puma's poem, "Show
Me Your Inner Goya"*

Keep Things Simple

There are so many different people to hate,
so I keep things simple and hate everyone.
I hate him for expiring, though I savor satisfaction
that my hate will last much longer
than the memories of his love.
I hate the people filing
past the casket lined with flowers.
We all came here to make quite sure
the scalawag is dead.
I leave the me who loved him
to rest upon his body.
Now I am someone entirely new.
A black dog, a broken heart.

First and last lines from Leigh Lucas' poem, "Dirtbag"

Always Someone

Self-consciousness has no currency here,
this here of security cameras,
spyglasses and eyeglasses,
family and neighbors
watching every move.
Never think nobody cares.
Loneliness has forgotten your address.

*First and last lines from Sarah Kay's poem, "In the House
With No Doors"*

Flight

You move through shards and splinters,
brown leaves swirling, falling, on the brambles,
a fluttering heart, wings worn to shreds.
Melodies I cannot hear
beckon you to unknown country.
I follow, you don't see me, know me.
I, a clod of half-baked mud,
and you, a bird in oblique flight.

First and last lines from Rosmarie Waldrop's poem, "A Valentine That Can't Be Sent"

Eyes

We sit in varying stages
of anesthesia staring
out the window, at the pictures
hanging on the wall,
anywhere but at the doctor
who pronounces certain doom
we've tried forever to avoid.
Tears blur choices other than
a line of mourners
whispering of tourniquets
and mouthing empty lies.
Glory hallelujah, angels
sing above the sadness.
We survey the rim of heaven
with our elastic eyes.

First and last lines from Tim Moder's poem, "Landscape with Fall of Civilization: Imaginings After Touring Chaco Canyon and Canyon de Chelly"

My Father's Death

My father's last breath is still the blade
that pares and cleaves me open.
I bleed cigars and Yukon Jack and armadillos.
Our time together, humor scrawled
on tattered barroom napkins.
I tell him what he missed, but he's not listening.
How to live knowing all of this will one day join him in
the dirt.

*First and last lines from Jade Cho's poem, "Three
Months Since"*

Looking for Something Higher

I dip an oar, I translate god
in rippled, stippled waters.
Moss-draped boughs and dragonflies
obscure my upward vision.
Perhaps in depths the heights are found.
I look for God in lilies.

First and last lines from Tim Moder's poem, "Loon"

Pray and Measure

Remind me
all my prayers were answered
the moment I started praying
for what I already have.
I need to stop to see
the length of a moment
that expands to hold
a thunderstorm, the moon.
Turn my tape measure
into a rosary that wraps
around my days.
Wasn't it death that taught me
to stop measuring my lifespan by length,
but by width?

First and last lines from Andrea Gibson's poem, "In the chemo room, I wear mittens made of ice so I don't lose my fingernails. But I took a risk today to write this down"

About the Author

Nolcha and her mother Sarah Erman

Nolcha Fox's poems have been curated in print and online journals. A best-selling author, her poetry books are available on Amazon and Dancing Girl Press. Nominated for Best Of The Net and Pushcart Prize multiple times. Editor of Chewers by Masticadores and LatinosUSA.

Website: writingaddiction2.wordpress.com/ and nolchafox2.wixsite.com/nolcha-s-written-wor/blog
Facebook: facebook.com/nolcha.fox/

www.ingramcontent.com/pod-product-compliance
Lightning Source LLC
Chambersburg PA
CBHW050909120626
46554CB00003B/1100